Tents

Written by Jo Windsor

In this book
you will see
tents.

You will see...

a tent for camping

a tent for a show

a work tent

a mountain tent

3

Look at this tent.

It is a small tent.

The man is up in the mountains.
It is very cold.

The man will sleep in the tent at night.
He will be warm in this tent.

This tent is small.

This tent is for people who work under the road.

This tent...

keeps the people dry   Yes? No?

keeps the people safe   Yes? No?

keeps the people warm   Yes? No?

These tents are small, too.
They are at the beach.

These tents are for...

playing in   Yes? No?

keeping the
sun out   Yes? No?

This tent has two rooms.

One room is for cooking.
One room is for sleeping.

At night the family will stay
in the forest and sleep in the tent.

The people are...

☺ happy   Yes? No?

☹ sad   Yes? No?

This tent is big.

It is in the desert.
People in the desert
can live in this tent.

The tent helps
keep the sun out.

At night it helps
keep them warm.

This is a very big tent.

This tent is like a big, big room. The people are at a wedding.

The people will have food in the tent.

The people will dance in the tent, too.

This tent is very, very big.

This tent is for a show.

Lots of people
will go to the show.
The show will be in the tent.

The people at the
show will be...

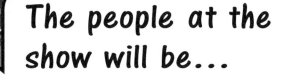 happy   Yes? No?

 sad   Yes? No?

This tent is for helping people. Some people are sick.

The doctors and nurses will help the people in this tent.

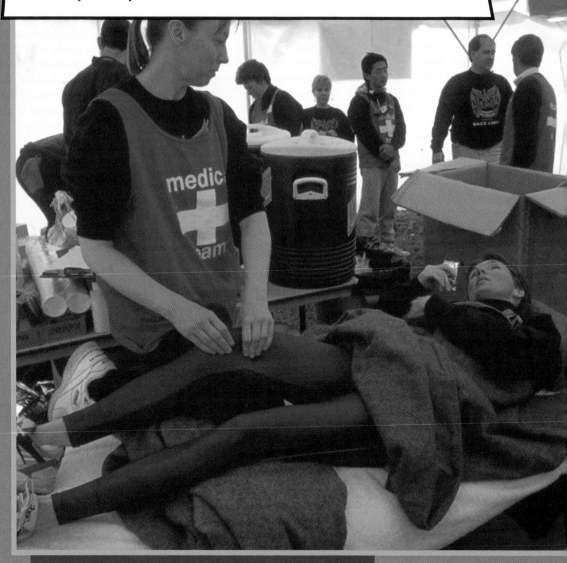

Index

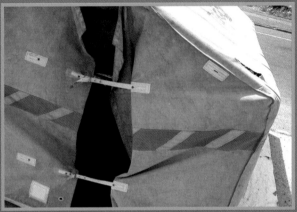

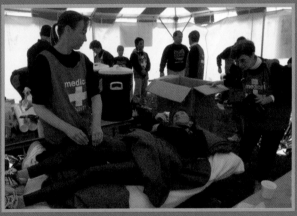

Word Bank

forest

mountains

night

road

sun